06/02

P9-AFR-618

WOMEN WHO WIN

Laila Ali

Cynthia Cooper

Lindsay Davenport

Mia Hamm

Martina Hingis

Chamique Holdsclaw

Marion Jones

Anna Kournikova

Michelle Kwan

Lisa Leslie

Gabrielle Reece

Dorothy "Dot" Richardson

Sheryl Swoopes

Venus & Serena Williams

CHELSEA HOUSE PUBLISHERS

WOMEN WHO WIN

Lindsay Davenport

John McCann

Introduction by
HANNAH STORM

CHELSEA HOUSE PUBLISHERS
Philadelphia

Frontis: With the encouragement of tennis legend Billy Jean King, Lindsay stepped onto the court with confidence and won Olympic gold. Only the third U.S. woman to do so, Lindsay put herself into the history books. Here she is at the medal awards ceremony.

CHELSEA HOUSE PUBLISHERS

Editor in Chief: Sally Cheney
Director of Production: Kim Shinners
Production Manager: Pamela Loos
Art Director: Sara Davis
Production Editor: Diann Grasse

Staff for Lindsay Davenport
Editor: Sally Cheney
Associate Editor: Benjamin Kim
Associate Art Director: Takeshi Takahashi
Layout by D&G Limited.

The Chelsea House World Wide Web address is http://www.chelseahouse.com

First Printing

1 3 5 7 9 8 6 4 2

Library of Congress Cataloging-in-Publication Data

McCann, John T. (John Thomas), 1972–
   Lindsay Davenport / John T. McCann.
     p. cm. – (Women who win)
   ISBN 0-7910-6527-8 (alk. paper)
     1. Davenport, Lindsay—Juvenile literature 2. Tennis players —United
   States—Biography—Juvenile literature. [1. Davenport, Lindsay. 2. Tennis
   players. 3. Women—Biography.] I.Title. II. Series.

   GV994.D38M33 2001
   796.342'092—dc21
   [B]   2001028908

CONTENTS

WOMEN WHO WIN

Hannah Storm
NBC Studio Host

You go girl! Women's sports are the hottest thing going right now, with the 1900s ending in a big way. When the U.S. team won the 1999 Women's World Cup, it captured the imagination of all sports fans and served as a great inspiration for young girls everywhere to follow their dreams.

That was just the exclamation point on an explosive decade for women's sports—capped off by the Olympic gold medals for the U.S. women in hockey, softball, and basketball. All the excitement created by the U.S. national basketball team helped to launch the Women's National Basketball Association (WNBA), which began play in 1997. The fans embraced the concept, and for the first time, a successful and stable women's professional basketball league was formed.

I was the first ever play-by-play announcer for the WNBA—a big personal challenge. Broadcasting, just like sports, had some areas with limited opportunities for women. There have traditionally not been many play-by-play opportunities for women in sports television, so I had no experience. To tell you the truth, the challenge I faced was a little scary! Sometimes we are all afraid that we might not be up to a certain task. It is not easy to take risks, but unless we push ourselves we will stagnate and not grow.

Here's what happened to me. I had always wanted to do play-by-play earlier in my career, but I had never gotten the opportunity. Not that I was unhappy—I had been given studio hosting assignments that were unprecedented for a woman and my reputation was well established in the business. I was comfortable in my role . . . plus I had just had my first baby. The last thing I needed to do was suddenly tackle a new skill on national television and risk being criticized (not to mention, very stressed out!). Although I had always wanted to do play-by-play, I turned down the assignment twice, before reluctantly agreeing to give it a try. During my hosting stint of the NBA finals that year, I traveled back and forth to WNBA preseason games to practice play-by-play. I was on 11 flights in 14 days to seven different cities! My head was spinning and it was no surprise that I got sick. On the day of the first broadcast, I had to have shots just so I could go on the air without throwing up. I felt terrible and nervous, but I survived my first game. I wasn't very good but gradually, week by week,

I got better. By the end of the season, the TV reviews of my work were much better—USA Today called me "most improved."

During that 1997 season, I witnessed a lot of exciting basketball moments, from the first historic game to the first championship, won by the Houston Comets. The challenge of doing play-by-play was really exciting and I loved interviewing the women athletes and seeing the fans' enthusiasm. Over one million fans came to the games; my favorite sight was seeing young boys wearing the jerseys of female players—pretty cool. And to think I almost missed out on all of that. It reinforced the importance of taking chances and not being afraid of challenges or criticism. When we have an opportunity to follow our dreams, we need to go for it!

Thankfully, there are now more opportunities than ever for women in sports (and other areas, like broadcasting). We thank women, like those in this series, who have persevered despite lack of opportunities—women who have refused to see their limitations. Remember, women's sports has been around a long time. Way back in 396 B.C. Kyniska, a Spartan princess, won an Olympic chariot race. Of course, women weren't allowed to compete, so she was not allowed to collect her prize in person. At the 1996 Olympic games in Atlanta, Georgia, over 35,600 women competed, almost a third more than in the previous Summer Games. More than 20 new women's events have been added for the Sydney, Australia, Olympics in 2000. Women's collegiate sports continues to grow,spurred by the 1972 landmark legislation Title IX, which states that "no person in the United States shall, on the basis of sex, be excluded from participation in, be denied the benefits of, or be subjected to discrimination under any educational program or activity receiving federal financial assistance." This has set the stage for many more scholarships and opportunities for women, and now we have professional leagues as well. No longer do the most talented basketball players in the country have to go to Europe or Asia to earn a living.

The women in this series did not have as many opportunities as you have today. But they were persistent through all obstacles, both on the court and off. I can tell you that Cynthia Cooper is the strongest woman I know. What is it that makes Cynthia and the rest of the women included in this series so special? They are not afraid to share their struggles and their stories with us. Their willingness to show us their emotions, open their hearts, bare their souls, and let us into their lives is what, in my mind, separates them from their male counterparts. So accept this gift of their remarkable stories and be inspired. Because you, too, have what it takes to follow your dreams.

1

THE "MAJOR" PROBLEM

It was time for Lindsay Davenport to prove herself. Coming close just wasn't good enough anymore.

She was 22 years old and had been a professional tennis player for five years. The knock against her was that she'd never won a big match, what's known in tennis as "winning a major" or "winning a Grand Slam."

Prior to 1998, Lindsay had competed in three Grand Slam semifinals. But not once had she taken home the title.

"I think the mindset of the public and the media is that if you don't win a Grand Slam, you're not a great player," Davenport said. "I don't agree with that. I think Grand Slams are a true test, a very difficult test. But if it doesn't happen, I'm [still] going to look back at myself as a great player."

That's a good attitude. But it's also the typical response given when reporters cram notebooks and microphones in an athlete's face, because nobody enters a game aiming to lose. While there are lessons to be learned from setbacks, athletes are best defined as those who compete to win. Victory is never guaranteed. But it's always the goal.

The sweet taste of victory. Lindsay kisses her 1998 U.S. Open trophy. She beat Martina Hingis in straight sets, 6-3 and 7-5, to take the title.

Victory was obtainable at the 1998 U.S. Open. Lindsay was playing with a sore elbow, but she looked great on the court. Also, the U.S. Open was one of those major tournaments the critics claimed she couldn't win, and a victory here would silence them.

"Everything is flowing," she said, her confidence brimming. "The ball is coming off my racket cleanly. If I've ever been in a zone, this is it."

The early rounds of the tournament were a breeze, and Lindsay found herself in the semifinals. If there ever was a time to say "been there, done that," then this was it, because the semis were familiar territory for Lindsay. It was the hump she never could get over, the bridge she always failed to cross.

It was the place where Lindsay always came up short. And to make things tougher this time, she would have to go swing for swing with the talented Venus Williams, a very graceful girl with long legs and long arms that allowed her to cover the entire court with ease. But the smoothness of Venus's game contained a streak of power that could strike at any time. You can't just show up and expect to beat Venus Williams. You've got to come ready to play, and even then a tough match is guaranteed.

"If I'm playing well, I'm going to win it," Lindsay said. "If I'm not, I'm not going to win it."

Her analysis was simple and accurate. But also hanging in the balance were the words of Lindsay's critics, those who kept reminding her about how she always folded whenever it was time to excel in a Grand Slam tournament. Never mind the success it takes to play tennis at a consistently high level year after year in order to even advance in these extremely competitive tournaments. All critics care about is the championship. According to them, anything less than first place ranks with failure.

It is an unfortunate way to measure success. But it is the way things are judged in the world of big-time sports: Everybody loves a winner. And here was Lindsay with another opportunity to come before her doubters, another chance to either choke or be champion.

She cleared the hurdle! And at last, Lindsay Davenport was in the finals of a major tournament. After knocking at the door of a major victory so many times in the past, she finally had stepped over the threshold.

But almost still wasn't good enough. Lindsay understood that. She was well aware of the tremendous challenge of squaring off in the championship match against the top-ranked player in women's tennis, Martina Hingis. She was four years younger than Lindsay, but Martina already had established herself as one of the game's elite players.

"If I lose, I'll hear 'She'll never win one,'" Lindsay said, very mindful of the doubters who didn't think she was championship material. "For me, I just keep the attitude like every year's gotten better. If it's not meant to be tomorrow, I've got a great shot next year. But I know I'm going for it. This has been my dream, to win the U.S. Open."

Finally, that championship attitude was bursting out. It was always there. But now Lindsay was vocalizing it, openly expressing her desire to take home a Grand Slam tournament title.

Playing for the pure love of the game, Lindsay faced Martina Hingis in the finals of the U.S. Open in 1998. Maintaining a positive attitude has always been a key ingredient in Lindsay's style—and her victories.

But it wasn't like Martina Hingis was going to just roll over and hand the match to Lindsay. No, Martina was the top-ranked player in the world. There was too much on the line to be on her heels simply because Lindsay happened to be playing so well. She would respect Lindsay. But Lindsay had better come ready to play.

On the day of the match, about an hour before facing Martina, Lindsay was in the locker room, getting focused. The telephone rang. It was Mary Jo Fernandez, a good friend of Lindsay's but also a fellow tennis player who had been in tough matches herself.

Mary Jo offered some heartfelt words to her buddy, telling Lindsay about the 1993 French Open. Mary Jo lost in the finals there and just shrugged it off. She figured she'd get another shot. But she didn't. To which she emphasized how important it was for Lindsay to make the most of her opportunity at the 1998 U.S. Open. It wasn't to add pressure—then again, it was, but just enough to make Lindsay appreciate the moment and come out swinging. And did she ever!

Lindsay dominated. She won the match in straight sets, becoming the first U.S.-born woman to capture the crown since the great Chris Evert claimed it in 1982. But more impressive than that was how she secured the victory. Toward the end of the match, Martina Hingis had managed to get a looping drop shot over the net. That meant Lindsay needed to cover quite a bit of ground to get to the ball.

In years past, this would have been an easy point for Martina. That's because Lindsay would not even have made a play on the ball, back when she was heavier and unsure of herself. But the 1998 U.S. Open saw the new and improved version of Lindsay Davenport—a much lighter, quicker, and more confident player.

As the ball dropped once in the near court, Lindsay dashed toward the net with a flash of speed. She was so swift as she charged forward, much faster than at any other time up to that point in her career. Lindsay cocked back her racket and smacked the ball with tremendous force. Martina just watched. It was all she could do, as if someone had smeared glue on the bottom of her shoes.

Basically frozen in her tracks, Martina didn't even swing at the ball, ending the match. Lindsay had done what so many others said she couldn't. By putting behind past losses,

After her victory against Swiss pro Martina Hingis, Lindsay offers a hug and a word of congratulations to her opponent. Good sportsmanship is important to Lindsay, who never engages in "trash-talking" before or after a match.

she had pulled off an incredible breakthrough performance. Everything seemed to fall right into place for Lindsay. It was her time and, at last, she was a Grand Slam champion.

"My first Grand Slam final, my first match point, and I think I played a great point," said Lindsay. "I have tried so hard to get to a Grand Slam. I have tried so hard to do the best I can. I'm not the most unbelievable athlete."

Instead, Lindsay is someone who works hard. She's not the most gifted player in women's tennis. She's not the quickest. But Lindsay Davenport works as hard as anybody. "I never thought I'd be No. 1," she said. "I always watched Martina [Navratilova], Chris [Evert], Steffi [Graf] and Monica [Seles] with a different kind of respect."

All of those women were champions. They were extraordinary players, absolute superstars in women's tennis. "I idolized them all. I thought I'd have a successful career, and I wanted to win a Grand Slam," said Lindsay. "But I didn't necessarily think I could."

2

FIRST SERVE

She picked up a tennis racket at age 6. Which was odd, because Lindsay Davenport's parents and two sisters played volleyball. For some reason, though, Lindsay preferred the bounce of the fuzzy, green balls.

At first, tennis was just something for Lindsay to do after school. But things soon began to get serious. Lindsay took a great liking to the game, discovering she was pretty good at getting the ball over the net.

"You normally start playing volleyball at ten, so when I got to that age, I had already been playing tennis for three years. All my family was into volleyball, but I liked tennis and I kind of just stuck with it."

Lindsay's mom enrolled her in tennis lessons at a clinic near their home in Southern California. A man named Robert Lansdorp ran the clinic. He was well-known for his ability to teach tennis, and Lindsay figured she could learn from him. So she asked for private lessons.

Mr. Lansdorp said no.

Lindsay asked again the next day. The answer was still no, and she burst into tears. It was much like a child in a

While still in high school, Lindsay developed her talents as a player, entering the pro circuit in 1993 at the age of 17.

this dad couldn't play organized sports—maybe he had to work a job after school to help out on the family farm. So now that he has a child of his own, the father tries to relive what could have been by trying to make the child's success his own.

In recent years, there have been many news reports of parents who go to Little League games and lose control when things don't go their kid's way. These are the parents who fuss at the umpires and referees. They yell at the coaches. At times, they get nose-to-nose with other parents. And in some instances, they even yell at their own kid.

Lindsay's parents—especially her mother, Ann—had a more hands-off approach. Oh, they were there for their daughter if she needed them. But for the most part, Lindsay's parents chose to let her develop into an independent woman simply by granting her some independence.

"I just always wanted Lindsay to make her own decisions and her own mistakes," says Ann. "It's her life, and it's her career."

With the support of her parents, Lindsay could have chosen to play another sport besides tennis. Or she could have chosen to not play sports at all. Many young athletes have no choice in the matter. Their parents pretty much force them to play, and these are situations where the kid is pushed and pushed to excel and improve. Never mind that the kid absolutely hates what he or she is doing. But in order to please mom and dad, the child keeps quiet and takes the field.

"A racquet was not put in my hand at one or two years of age," said Lindsay. "I wasn't doing sit-ups or sprints at age three or four. I got into

Playing against third-ranked Arantxa Sanchez Vicario of Spain in the 1996 Olympics was a big challenge for Lindsay. But she played hard and kept her confidence and focus throughout the match.

tennis honestly because my mom wanted to give me something to do after school and she put me in a tennis program, which I started playing in and I just loved it."

Lindsay was just a normal kid who liked doing what normal kids do. Unfortunately, that also meant facing the same ups and downs as any other young person.

Sure, Lindsay was a big-time professional athlete. Her popularity was growing. But she also was a typical teenager with typical teenage problems—issues that would bring the rising star to one of the lowest times in her young life.

3

STICKS AND STONES

While Lindsay chose to stay in public school when her family moved to Murrieta, California, the idea of getting a private tutor actually might not have seemed like such a bad thing. Here she was in the 11th grade, almost a high school senior. She had her friends. They all had their favorite places to hang out. Then Lindsay's dad decides to pack up and move the family.

"It was the worst thing ever," said Lindsay.

But she went. Lindsay didn't speak to her dad for a month. Life had to go on, though. There was schoolwork. There were new friends to meet. Plus, Lindsay was a tennis pro, so there were tournaments to play and hopefully win. But things just weren't the same. And little did she know that things were about to get worse.

After more than 25 years of marriage, Lindsay's parents decided to divorce. The relationship had been crumbling over the years and, sure, all parents have disagreements from time to time. There may even be moments when moms and dads fuss and fight, which never is nice to see. But what's worse is when it leads to divorce.

After her parents divorced, Lindsay turned to junk food to mask the pain and guilt she was feeling. Before long, she had reached nearly 200 pounds, and was very sensitive about people's comments on her size.

"My parents were married for 26 years, and all of a sudden they're not speaking," said Lindsay. "I was worried about my mom being alone."

At this point, Lindsay had finished high school and was living by herself. But she called her mother every day to make sure everything was OK. Tennis was Lindsay's job, but nothing was more important than her mom. Besides, Lindsay felt like the whole divorce mess was her fault.

"I felt like I had abandoned them, that it wouldn't have happened if I had stayed home."

The divorce was like a heavy rock on Lindsay's shoulders, and the whole situation weighed on her tremendously, even affecting her play on the court. Her 1995 ranking dropped from No. 7 to No. 12. And a lot of that had to do with feelings of guilt, which would lead her to face an issue she had struggled with all her life.

Behind her back, the other players called her "Dump Truck." Either that or "Linebacker Lindsay."

These were professional tennis players saying these things, mind you. Yet they chose to stoop to the level of name-calling. What's worse, Lindsay Davenport was adding fuel to their fiery remarks.

"A lot of my gaining weight was guilt."

Lindsay was referring to her parent's divorce. She thought it was her fault—that her traveling all over the country, even around the world, was the reason her mom and dad split up. She felt that "it wouldn't have happened if I had stayed home."

So she turned to food. In particular, junk food—potato chips and sugary cereal. Some-

times, Lindsay wouldn't even be hungry, but she still would eat. It was an attempt to mask the pain she was feeling inside.

Some people abuse drugs. Others become alcoholics. Lindsay dealt with the pressure by overeating, and before long, she had ballooned to more than 200 pounds.

"I don't care how tall you are," she said, speaking honestly about her problem. "That's heavy."

Lindsay is nearly six feet, three inches tall. In a way, this was the problem. It always had been, because Lindsay routinely found herself standing out. In her opinion, she was standing out for the wrong reason. Think about the NBA's Shaquille O'Neal in relation to the other players in the league. Shaq always stands out as the big guy, which is a huge advantage in basketball.

But most female tennis players are under six feet tall. They are small and petite, and they wear cute dresses that show off their well-toned, but little, legs.

In her struggles with her weight, Lindsay envied some of the other thinner players, like the Williams sisters, Anna Kournikova, and Martina Hingis.

Lindsay has big legs. She's big-boned.

Unfortunately, Lindsay wasn't thick-skinned. When people talked about her size, it hurt. Even when nothing was said, Lindsay's mind always seemed to be fixed on what others were thinking.

Lindsay hardly had a choice in the matter, with her father being 6 feet 8 inches tall. Her mother is relatively tall for a woman, at 5 feet 10 inches. The problem with Lindsay was she had failed to view her height as an asset, unlike Venus Williams, who, at 6 feet 1, is nearly as tall as Lindsay. But Venus didn't weigh 200 pounds. No, at 160 pounds, Venus Williams was slim. She was cat-quick and able to dash to any spot on the court to make a play on the ball.

What must not be forgotten is Lindsay still was very young at the time. Sure, she was a pro. But Lindsay still was maturing, caught in a struggle to fit in with everybody else. She was trying to find herself.

It's the very reason many experts warn against young athletes becoming professionals too soon. Sports such as football and basketball sometimes have kids turning pro only after a few years of college. Every now and then, a high school basketball player makes the jump to the professional ranks.

The concern is the player won't be mature enough to handle the rigors of pro sports. Physically, the bodies of young players often haven't fully developed. Couple that with maintaining a demanding sports schedule against players who are more physically mature, and the potential for injuries increases. That can cut a player's career short.

Then there's the concern that a young athlete isn't mature enough mentally to handle the pressures of pro sports. While football, basketball, and baseball players generally make it past 12th grade before becoming pros, tennis is a sport where players often compete professionally before finishing high school—which can take its toll on a player.

Tennis phenomenon Jennifer Capriati, born March 29, 1976, is roughly the same age as Lindsay Davenport. She turned pro in 1990, three years before Lindsay. At 13 years old, Jennifer was the youngest tennis player ever to become a professional.

"Even though I'm going to be playing older ladies, when I'm out there playing, I'm as old as they are," she said. "I have no fear."

Jennifer was young and bold, and like most kids, she had a recklessness about her. It is as if nothing in life scares them because they haven't been living long enough to see all the bad things waiting for them if they make a wrong move.

Often, when young people make up their minds to do something, there's no discouraging them. So although Jennifer had been told about the tremendous demands of professional tennis, her mind was made up. The result was physical injury and mental burnout—the very thing that happened to Tracy Austin and Andrea Jaeger, both young tennis stars whose careers were soon frustrated by nagging injuries. In fact, because the problems with her feet and back were so severe, Tracy Austin's career was over by the time she was 19 years old.

As Jennifer Capriati demonstrated similar success, tennis experts wondered if injuries soon would creep in and cripple her young career.

"Why does everybody think it's going to happen to me?" she wondered.

Defending her 2000 Australian Open title in 2001 was a real challenge for Lindsay. Her opponent in the semifinal match was Jennifer Capriati, a hard-driving competitor with her eyes on the prize. Here Capriati returns the ball at center court.

The simple answer was that it had happened before, and the tennis experts turned out to be right. After winning a gold medal in the 1992 Olympics, Jennifer had problems with bone chips and tendinitis in her elbow.

From there, things went downhill. Jennifer moved away from her parents' home. Then she announced her decision to leave tennis in order to finish high school, only to drop out instead. She would later get arrested on drug charges and begin a rehabilitation program.

Jennifer Capriati was only 18 years old.

The point here is to underscore the potential pressures of professional sports on a young person. While there's money to be made and success to be gained, the priorities of life must remain in focus. That's what Lindsay Davenport had to come to grips with.

Like Lindsay, Jennifer's parents also divorced. That left plenty of room to shift blame. But in the end, Jennifer decided to take responsibility and get her life together. Before long, she was back on the tennis courts, doing what she loved.

For Lindsay, it was during the mid-1990s that the world seemed to be caving in on her. There was her parents' divorce, followed by her feelings of guilt about the breakup. While Lindsay didn't abuse her body with drugs, there was her problem with overeating. As she began gaining weight, there were feelings of envy toward players like Venus Williams, who were smaller and better suited to their tennis outfits. It was a life of self-doubt and Lindsay was sick of it.

It was time to change. It was time to stop wearing flat shoes to try to look shorter. It was time to stop walking bent over in hopes of hiding a few inches from her tall body, as if nobody would notice.

It was time to take control and stop blaming herself.

It was time to get in shape.

Lindsay knew a guy named Robert Van't Hof, so she got in touch with him. He had been around the game of tennis for a long time, and he was someone to whom Lindsay could turn for advice. That made him the perfect person to become her personal trainer.

She began to change her training and diet. Which is not to say Lindsay starved herself. While the workouts were intense, the meals were balanced. Lindsay simply got rid of the junk food and cut back on the portions.

There were sprints along the beach in the thick sand. That helped her leg strength and endurance. Lindsay played basketball to improve her footwork. She ran stadium steps, lifted weights, and burned even more calories on the treadmill, all of which resulted in two significant achievements in Lindsay's life.

She lost weight.

And the 20-year-old struck gold.

Working with personal trainer Robert Van't Hof proved to be good medicine for Lindsay. She was committed to losing weight, and by eating better and training harder, she was able to drop 30 pounds.

4

GOOD AS GOLD

Thirty pounds lighter and her parents' divorce behind her, a tremendous burden had been lifted from Lindsay's shoulders. She was ready to get back into the swing of things, especially on the tennis court.

It was 1996, an Olympic year, and Lindsay had earned a spot on the team. She always had dreamed of being an Olympian. Her dad played volleyball in the 1968 Olympics, so representing her country in the 1996 games was another milestone. And most important, Lindsay was back to playing exceptional tennis and having fun doing so.

The world's best tennis players were at the Olympics that year in Atlanta, Georgia. Lindsay had to be considered among the elite, because she managed to make it to the final match.

What an extraordinary accomplishment to have arrived at this shining moment. Through her amazing determination, Lindsay had transformed her body into a machine. She would always be tall. But now her body was tight and toned, free of excess weight.

The same players she once envied now had to take notice of her, especially now with a chance to bring home a gold medal. To do so, she would have to get past Arantxa

Lindsay has some fun off the court too. Here, she throws out the first pitch at a Yankees-Angels baseball game.

Sanchez Vicario, a Spanish player ranked third best in the world.

"This is going to be the biggest match of my life, for sure," Lindsay said. "I've been seeing all the athletes up there for the last week and a half getting their gold medals and hearing the anthem. I hope I can do the same."

The Olympics are entirely different from any other sporting event. They give athletes a chance to compete and demonstrate their skills on a world stage. While doing well at the Olympics can be financially beneficial afterward, the spirit of the games is not about money. Instead, athletes chase gold medals. In fact, even the second-place silver medals and third-place bronze medals are precious prizes.

Because the Olympics come around just once every four years, for many, they represent a once-in-a-lifetime opportunity. That means pressure. But it's a place where athletes can achieve a place in history. Young men and women spend their entire lives training for chance to represent their countries. It's why superstars from the National Basketball Association jump at the chance to compete in the Olympics. Their million-dollar contracts are nice. But no amount of money can buy a gold medal.

Lindsay Davenport understood that.

"She was always taught that it's an honor to be picked to represent your country, that it's the patriotic thing to do," said Lindsay's mother, Ann Davenport.

One of the greatest scenes in American sports is the Olympic award ceremonies. With a hand over the heart, athletes stand tall as the national anthem plays. Tears sometimes well up in their eyes from the thought of having made good on a very unique opportunity. But for Lindsay to get the gold medal placed around her neck, she had to do something no one enjoys: defeat a close friend.

There was a bump in the middle of Lindsay's road to Olympic glory, and her name was Mary Jo Fernandez. She was Lindsay's close friend, and the two had to play against each other. It was the luck of the draw—simply the way the match-ups worked out.

It was a painful experience, to say the least. After defeating Mary Jo, Lindsay went to the locker room and cried.

"I was playing someone who's my best friend," she said. "I don't want to go out there and see her lose."

It was one of those situations where it was nothing personal, just business. And at this point, there was some unfinished business—beating Arantxa Sanchez Vicario.

Arantxa had been sizzling on the court. In addition, before coming to the Olympics, she had beaten Lindsay the last five times they played. Now ranked higher than Lindsay here at the Olympics, the advantage, it would seem, had to be with Arantxa.

But Lindsay had her supporters. A lot of people believed in her. One such person was her U.S. Olympic Team coach, Billie Jean King, who had been a tremendous player herself.

"This could be a huge turning point for her," King said.

That type of encouragement can do a lot for anybody. And when the encouragement comes from someone as well-respected as Billie Jean King, and when it gets showered upon an athlete at one of the biggest moments of her career, it can offer the mental edge needed to come out on top. Which Lindsay did, emerging victorious in front of a crowd of 12,000 people.

Perhaps the most painful challenge of Lindsay's career was having to go up against her close friend Mary Jo Fernandez (shown here) at the 1996 Olympic Games. She knew that being a pro meant she would have to play her best game, even against a friend. After defeating Fernandez, Lindsay returned to the locker room and cried.

"[Billy Jean King] told me three weeks ago that I could win gold here," said Lindsay. "I'll never be able to thank her enough for giving me that kind of confidence and support."

The talent was always there. Lindsay just needed that extra push, that added word of encouragement. She needed somebody to tell her to just do it.

"The only thing we talked about," said Billie Jean King, "is what a turning point this could be for her."

It certainly was that. Now brimming with confidence, Lindsay felt as if she could handle whatever came her way. That's not to be confused with being conceited or stuck up, because Lindsay has never been that kind of person. But winning the gold medal just seemed to do something for her. Considering how she had to cope with her parents' divorce, and taking into account how she battled to overcome her weight problem and get in shape, Lindsay's Olympic win was the right spark at the right time.

Up to that point in 1996, only two American women had won Olympic gold medals in tennis. Helen Wills did it in 1924. Jennifer Capriati brought home gold in 1992. So Lindsay's win was a major event.

"This is the most proud I've ever been in my life," she said. "This means everything to me. No matter what happens in my life, I'll always be a gold medal winner."

Lindsay was right where she wanted to be. With a gold medal to her credit, she was playing great. Her weight was under control, so she also looked great. And through it all, she never became one of those screaming, selfish athletes who make millions of dollars and seem to create as many headaches for those around them.

"I don't play tennis to show off or to play in front of a lot of people," she said. "I play tennis because I love to play tennis, and I always said whether it's on Court 15 at a public park or on Centre Court at a Grand Slam, I just like to play."

She does get paid. In fact, Lindsay gets paid a lot. She has earned more than $11 million since 1993 doing something she would do for free if she had to. But the riches don't define her.

Although Lindsay lost her Australian Open title to Jennifer Capriati in 2001, she remains hopeful about the future. Here she congratulates Capriati on her win.

"I put most of my money in the bank," Lindsay said. "I know if I really want something I can buy it. But I don't really want that much."

It's this very attitude she carries onto the tennis court. At a time when pro athletes are expected to be flashy, Lindsay Davenport is no show-off.

"You don't have to give this false attitude off," she said. "You don't have to tell everybody how great or tough you are. You can treat people with respect. You don't change just because you're good at something you do."

But many athletes do just that. According to sports psychologist Mark Anshel, "We wrongly make the assumption that because an athlete is a professional earning a great deal of money, that an athlete has the emotional maturity to make the right choices in life."

Anshel said most people fail to realize that many athletes suffer from low self-esteem. Never mind all the boasting and taunting and finger-pointing they do.

"The boasting is a cover up," he said. "People who are really confident do not need to boast. They let their performance speak for them."

That's what real winners do. They let their actions speak louder than their words. It's the way true champions carry themselves. That's Lindsay Davenport.

"I don't really like the spotlight. I don't want to grab the attention."

Other players do. And that's fine, if that's their approach. But if trash talking is the crowning jewel that marks one's ultimate success, then Lindsay is contented to stay right where she is.

"I like the position I'm in," she said, not at all envious of the other players.

"They're all outspoken," Lindsay said. "They all have distinct attitudes. Their personalities are very much out there. They're kind of in-your-face."

Lindsay looks beyond all the bragging. She respects the other players. They're professionals just like her, and they're entitled to project themselves as they please. In fact, many athletes are rewarded for their boastful attitudes with big contracts that allow them to make money advertising everything from sportswear to soft drinks. But again, if trash talking is the criteria, then don't look for Lindsay to have anything to do with it.

"I hold nothing against them," she said. "Everybody is their own person. But some of the things they say and do sometimes I laugh about, because they try to give this impression that they're so confident, yet everything they do kind of shows that they're really not. To me, a truly confident person doesn't need to try and tell everybody how great they are."

What can't be forgotten is Lindsay wasn't always so confident herself. For most of her teenage years, she was a girl who struggled to cope with her size. She was taller than everybody else. She was bigger than everybody else. And she knew it, and it hurt.

"I had to build up the confidence and get to the point where I felt really good about myself. It's amazing to go through that and to think that so much for me personally was mental as much as it was physical. And to think that I could become such a positive person and really believe in myself."

It was a remarkable accomplishment. Lindsay's mother used to get on her case for her poor posture. As Lindsay would hunch over to hide her tall body. Unfortunately, it would be years later—after finishing high school and a few years into her pro career—before the message finally sank in, that there's nothing wrong with looking different.

If there were no tall people, there would be no short people. If there were no short people, there would be no tall people, and so forth. Everybody has a place, and everybody's place is worth something.

"I think everything I've gone through is extremely ordinary. I mean, especially with teenage girls being heavy and trying to lose weight and trying to fit in and all these kind of things," Lindsay said. "I hope people can relate to me."

Other players on the women's pro tour noticed Lindsay's new vibe. She was still the low-key person who didn't seek the spotlight. But now there was a confidence about her, an inner glow.

"She's mentally so much stronger," said Martina Hingis, one of the bright, young tennis stars who has spent a great deal of time in the No. 1 slot. "Before [Lindsay] would be very moody. You would just see on her face that she was not happy with what she was doing, and she would give up much easier."

Now Lindsay had that desire to win. There was a new fuel to her fire. And it was time to chase another Grand Slam victory.

5

WINNING WIMBLEDON

Ask a professional football player about the most disappointing aspect of his career, and he probably will point to not winning a Super Bowl. This big football player would look you square in the eye, then he would describe all the great things he accomplished throughout his career. He would talk about the truckload of individual honors and accomplishments that he has gained. But let him keep talking, and sooner or later the conversation will come back to how he was never able to slide one of those big Super Bowl rings onto his finger.

A baseball player would say the same thing about the World Series. A basketball player dreams of nailing the big shot in the deciding game of the NBA Finals.

When it comes to tennis, the game's best players fix their eyes on England. What they envision is winning Wimbledon, which means prize money, of course. And there's the really huge trophy, which for the female players is a bowl. But to understand the history behind that bowl is to understand that Wimbledon is not just any ordinary tennis tournament.

Wimbledon's grass courts provide an added challenge for players accustomed to harder playing surfaces. The ball can take some tricky bounces on grass and players must be prepared to adjust their style to keep their winning edge.

While the men's championship competition began in 1877, female players didn't become part of Wimbledon until 1884. For both the men and women, Wimbledon back in those days, and tennis in general, was very different from the game that's played today. Namely, the opportunity to earn thousands and thousands of dollars for participating in a tennis tournament just wasn't there. That would change over time as Wimbledon grew to become the cream of the tennis crop. In fact, the kings, queens, and princes that make up British royalty have long been associated with Wimbledon—a tradition that continues today.

For women, the early days of tennis were dramatically different from modern times. For starters, they didn't wear shorts and T-shirts or skirts. Back during those days, the trendy fashion was long dresses that came down to the ankles. It was like wearing wedding clothes to the gym.

There were no Nikes or Reeboks or any other brand-named tennis shoes. These women played in high heels. They wore big hats, the kind you might see women wear to church.

As funny as that sounds, it was not out of the ordinary. Back in those days, tennis was a social game for women. They weren't encouraged to go all out on the tennis court and work up a big sweat. Women were to take it nice and easy, playing the game like the ladies they were. In fact, women actually used an underarm serve, a far cry from the powerful over-the-top serving style used by today's female players.

Limiting women tennis players to what was traditionally considered feminine began to change around 1886. That was the year when a 15-year-old named Lottie Dod stepped on the scene and won Wimbledon. She was very athletic and strongly built. She even played an exhibition match against a man in 1888. Lottie lost to this man, who had won Wimbledon many times before. But there was a rematch later in the year and she beat him.

"Ladies should learn to run and run their hardest too, not merely stride," said Lottie Dod. "They would find (if they tried) that many a ball, seemingly out of reach, could be returned with ease; but instead of running hard they go a few steps and exclaim, 'Oh, I can't' and stop."

The women's game would continue to evolve. The players would become stronger and more athletic. The women would begin using the overhand serve, and the tennis dresses would become shorter, allowing more flexibility.

Which brings us to modern times, where it's socially acceptable for women to sweat hard and dive for tough shots just like the men. It's OK today for women to lift weights and build their muscles, while still retaining their femininity.

What's interesting to note about a player like Lindsay Davenport are her similarities to players from the old days. She's sort of a throwback, and that's not a jab at Lindsay in any way. It's actually a compliment to her conservative approach to the game.

By now, it's well established that Lindsay is not a trash-talker. Nor is she a show-off, not in her style of play or the way she dresses. That's what makes her a throwback.

Many players, good or bad, draw attention to themselves by wearing very tight, form-fitting tennis outfits. Lindsay keeps her clothes pretty loose, like the women of old.

Lindsay even wears a cap from time to time, although nothing like the huge hats they wore in Lottie Dod's day.

But more important that fashion, tennis comes down to getting the job done on the court. You can be the best-looking player out there. But if you're not on top of your game, you won't win—which is especially true at Wimbledon.

Wimbledon is played on a grass court, but not like the grass in your front yard. The grass on these courts is trimmed very, very low. It's like playing on green carpet. And because it's grass, the tennis ball responds differently. On hard surfaces, you get a true bounce, one that's easier to predict and smack. But on grass courts, the surface is softer so the bounce of the ball becomes tricky. The natural texture of grass already has lumps in it, and more are created during the course of the match as players shuffle around the court. Even the small lumps can cause the ball to bounce in an unexpected way, adding to the challenge.

Combine all of that history with all of the supremely talented athletes who play year after year at Wimbledon, and the importance of claiming this milestone of a tournament becomes overwhelmingly clear.

Lindsay had a shot in 1999.

For two weeks, she hustled and sweated, battling the best players in the world. Playing on grass had never been her strength. But somehow everything came together over those 14 days, because she found herself on Centre Court, a special playing area that most tennis facilities have. But the Centre Court at Wimbledon is particularly significant, mainly due to all of the remarkable history of the famous tournament.

And that's where Lindsay found herself, in the championship match at Wimbledon. To top it off, she was facing one of the most dominant players of all time—Steffi Graf, who already had won Wimbledon seven times!

As the tennis world focused in on the match, it seemed clear that the deck was stacked in favor of Steffi Graf. At 30 years old, she was mature. Playing at Centre Court would not rattle her nerves, because she was experienced. Steffi had played here before and she had won here before—many times.

On the other hand, Lindsay had never been in a Wimbledon final. This was the first one, and for a 23-year-old such as herself, it had to be pretty nerve-wracking. Sure, she'd won the U.S. Open the year prior to this moment. But this was Wimbledon. It was the big show, the tennis tournament of tennis tournaments. Lindsay had never made it past the Wimbledon quarterfinals in prior years. But now, here she was.

Adding drama to championship day was a rain delay in the middle of the match. It lasted 30 minutes, forcing both Steffi and Lindsay to wait it out.

Before long, the rain showers ceased. The players returned to the court and took a few warm-up swings. It was time to finish what they started. Such a delay can really affect the nerves of a younger player, because it allows time for doubts to damage concentration and confidence.

Lindsay would need nerves of steel. She would have to really focus and do all the little things it takes to win. If she could just stick to her game plan, she would be OK. If Lindsay could play smart tennis, while still being aggressive, then the cloudy weather wouldn't put a damper on her quest to conquer Wimbledon.

Lindsay got the job done. She served the ball well and she stayed focused, and Lindsay beat the tennis legend.

One of Lindsay's toughest opponents, German pro Steffi Graf in action at the 1999 French Open. Later that year, Lindsay defeated Graf to take the women's singles championship at Wimbledon.

"It was almost like a dream," said Lindsay.

The win at Wimbledon marked her second Grand Slam title. Just a few years before, Lindsay was the girl who couldn't win the big matches. Now, in her own time, she was proving everybody wrong.

"The victory at the U.S. Open was incredible because it was my first," she said, thinking back to all the times people said she'd never win a major tournament. Now here she was with two Grand Slams. Here she was with Wimbledon! "People who said I couldn't win the big one, I felt so much pride to tell them they were wrong."

It was as if people simply refused to truly acknowledge Lindsay's game, because she still wasn't getting the respect she deserved. During the first week of Wimbledon, the media basically paid her no mind. All the newspaper reporters and TV journalists seemed to want to speak to the more flashy players, as if Lindsay were just too plain or too boring.

"I don't create a lot of attention where I go, but for me that's not a bad thing," she said.

Instead, Lindsay just sort of minds her own business and does what she knows to do, which is to play good, solid tennis. She's not going to go out there and give you a lot of highlights. Lindsay is very capable of making big plays. But her game is best described as steady, and the next thing you know, Lindsay is the one holding up the trophy.

"When I won, I was almost more numb than in shock," she said. "I never thought that it would be my Wimbledon because I had struggled on this surface before." Not everyone plays well on the grass courts of Wimbledon. But it was the surface of the moment for Lindsay, and she mastered it.

"To win on two different surfaces means I'm a pretty good all-around player," Lindsay said, referring to her 1998 win on the hard courts of the U.S. Open. "And to come in here at 15-1 odds and to defy the experts on that, it just feels incredible. Maybe the media or other people might underestimate me, but I've always felt the players know what caliber player I am."

After Wimbledon, everybody knew what kind of player Lindsay was. Not only did she beat one of the games best champions, the win over Steffi Graf vaulted her into the No. 1 ranking.

But as is characteristic of Lindsay, individual awards and drawing attention to herself never have been the reason why she played the game. It's about getting the ball over the net and competing.

For Lindsay Davenport, tennis comes down to the history of the game and all of its rich tradition. "I'll take the Wimbledon championship any day over the No. 1 ranking," she said.

6

LIFE GOES ON

As awesome as it was, winning Wimbledon was bitter-sweet for Lindsay Davenport.

Make no mistake, there was nothing sad about holding up that big trophy while everybody cheered her victory at Centre Court. It was an incredible moment for Lindsay. She knew it, and she savored it.

But the match also brought to an end the spectacular Wimbledon career of Steffi Graf. "Basically, I won't be back," said Steffi, who was 30 years old at the time. "I won't be here as a player."

A month before Wimbledon, after winning her sixth French Open, Graf announced that it was her last time playing in that tournament, too. She had been at it for 17 years, one of the games toughest competitors. Steffi's last few year on the tennis circuit had been marked by a back injury, so it appeared as if Steffi was ready to close her locker for the last time.

"If she's not playing in the French or Wimbledon again, that means she's probably retiring some time this year,"

For pro tennis players there may be no greater reward than a win at England's Wimbledon tournament. On July 4, 1999 Lindsay earned that honor with a win over seven-time Wimbledon champ Steffi Graf. After the match, Graf retired from competition.

Lindsay said in 1999. "She's the greatest player who's probably ever played, but at the same time, I think it's really cool that she's been able to go out on her own."

Which raises the question of how long Lindsay herself will choose to keep swinging a tennis racket. In any job, there comes a time when your best years have long gone, and it's best to step aside and move on to other things.

The longevity of a career in professional sports is much shorter than that of most other occupations. While pro athletes generally make more money doing their jobs, the window of opportunity to be productive in their line of work is very narrow. That's why athletes must plan ahead. The smart ones realize that a No. 1 ranking today can be gone tomorrow.

"Things are going great right now," said Lindsay. "But I'm also realistic that they can't forever go this great. So you just have to enjoy it while it's here."

Emotionally, the tall blonde from California couldn't be better. She feels good on the tennis court. But more important than that, Lindsay feels good off the tennis court. She feels good about herself.

"I'm feeling so great," said Lindsay, finally comfortable at 6 feet 2 inches tall, 175 pounds. "I'm pretty confident this is what I'll be for the rest of my life. I just enjoy seeing the results. I'm very, very big-boned. No matter how thin I get, I'll never get below a size ten. I just have big legs."

It's a far cry from where Lindsay started. Before the confidence boost, she was actually so miserable she thought seriously about quitting tennis. The fat jokes were becoming too much for Lindsay to bear. She'd had just about all the insults she could take.

"Some people made it sound like all I did was sit around all day eating cheeseburgers."

Perhaps not cheeseburgers, but she was putting down a lot of food. Now, that eating problem is under control. No fad diets for Lindsay. She simply eats sensibly, meaning her favorite meal of beef stroganoff is not off–limits. Lindsay just doesn't pile as much on her plate.

"I've gotten real good at sharing food," said Lindsay. "I order one plate now for two people."

She can joke about it now. The ugly memories have faded. But at the time, each trip past a mirror was a painful reminder of what others saw. "It hurts when you're a teenager and people say you're too fat," she said before the 1998 U.S. Open. "Now I feel good about how I look, and I'm taking that out onto the court with me. My confidence level is at an all-time high."

It's so obvious.

"You see it in her whole game," said German tennis player Anke Huber. "When she's down, she's believing in herself all the time."

"She's wanting it more and working more," said Martina Hingis. "She lost weight and she's serving better."

"She's very, very confident and that's a big difference," said Aranxta Sanchez Vicario.

So tennis is under control.

Materially, Lindsay can afford to have almost anything she wants. She has made many millions of dollars playing tennis. Just for winning the Wimbledon singles title back in 1999, Lindsay got a check worth more than $600,000.

So money is not an issue. But there is one off-court concern that Lindsay thinks about more and more as the years go on.

"I would love to have a family at some point."

Marriage would be really sweet. Kids would

be the icing on the cake. For now, she plays peekaboo with her niece, a little girl named Kennedy. Lindsay also has two Rottweilers.

In her free time, Lindsay likes to kick back to the sounds of alternative music. She's an Atlanta Braves fan, and Lindsay also likes the New York Yankees and the Anaheim Mighty Ducks. When Lindsay gets free time, she enjoys spending it in the Bahamas. Hawaii is nice, too.

Lindsay's interests are wide-ranging like that. She likes a lot of different things. Soon enough, she'll have the time to pursue them.

"I'm looking forward to doing other things in my life when this career's over," said Lindsay. "I hope I can be a little bit bigger than just Lindsay Davenport, tennis player."

But right now, tennis takes top priority.

All the hype surrounding the millennium was kicked up a notch for Lindsay Davenport when she won the 2000 Australian Open. It was the first Grand Slam tournament of the year, and she beat Martina Hingis to win it. The victory ended Martina's three-year hold on the Australian Open title.

Now it was Lindsay's turn to defend the crown. So she headed back to the place knows as "The Land Down Under," where her previous success would matter little. With any sport, you're only as good as your last game. And while entering the 2001 Australian Open ranked as the tournament's second-best player, Lindsay still had to tie her shoes a little tighter and concentrate just as hard. She was the defending champ, and the best players in the world would be coming for her crown.

The first round was tough, but Lindsay hung on, beating Jelena Dokic. But there would be no time to rest in the second round,

Sailing to victory.
Lindsay sports her 2000
Australian Open trophy
on a gondola ride up the
Yarra River.

despite playing against an opponent she was expected to defeat.

The match was against a German named Greta Arn, who was ranked No. 146. Since Lindsay was ranked No. 2, she was expected to win. But that first-round match had taken a lot out of her, making this contest against Greta more grueling.

"I felt tired and a little sluggish today. I don't know if it's from finishing late the other night and having a little bit of a letdown after a match that had a lot of hype. It's tough to go from something really big to a match that you're supposed to win handily." No doubt about it, Lindsay was the heavy favorite, herself a top-five player against another who hadn't cracked the top 100. But there's something about big games that bring out the best in every athlete. It's during these times when the rankings are thrown out of the window. You just get out there and play.

Still, Lindsay held on, somehow finding enough strength to launch powerful serves that allowed her to stay in control. But Lindsay wasn't playing her best tennis, and she knew it.

"I'm a little bit away from my A-game right now," Lindsay said, "but the girls are getting better."

And they were coming for her title. Lindsay knew she had to get it in gear and do so in a hurry.

The next match was a piece of cake. Lindsay beat Silvia Farina Elia. The champ was finding her rhythm and getting into a nice groove.

"I'm a lot happier with the way I played," Lindsay said. "You can tell when you're hitting the ball cleanly and well, even when you might not win every point. I was hitting with more power and depth and all that good stuff I've been lacking the last couple of matches."

She'd have to keep it up. Her fourth-round opponent was the tournament's No. 15 seed, meaning the competition was getting tougher, the pressure to win more intense. Kim Clijsters was hitting the ball extremely well, and if Lindsay still was looking for her A-game, this definitely was the time to find it.

"It will be a tough match against Kim," said Lindsay. "It doesn't seem so long ago that I was the youngest on tour. Now, at 24, I'm one of the oldest and there's a heap of young players playing well and hitting the ball hard."

It didn't matter. Lindsay was too much for Kim and racked up another win.

Up next was Anna Kournikova, the Russian whose beauty is talked about more than her backhand. Ranked eighth in the tournament, Kournikova came out swinging pretty and hitting hard. Her power caused Lindsay to scramble a bit, but Lindsay settled down and unleashed her tremendous serve. She was in the zone, hitting the ball powerfully and accurately. Lindsay poured it on and went on to win.

"I think I'm getting better as it goes on."

That set up a rematch of the previous year's semifinal against Jennifer Capriati who, understandably, had a score to settle. Lindsay knew what she had to do. "We had a tough match last year." This was no time to let up. The title was on the line.

Unfortunately, Lindsay didn't bring her A-game. She wasn't sharp that day. The 12th-seeded Jennifer Capriati dusted Lindsay, giving the defending champion a taste of her own medicine. The power Lindsay used to crush everybody else was turned on her by Jennifer's aggressive play.

"Her balls were coming extremely hard, so then it's also hard to kind of do what you want with the ball," said Lindsay, who served poorly and simply made too many mistakes.

To her credit, at least Lindsay lost to the person who would go on to win the tournament. But for an athlete, losing is never the desired result, especially for top players at Lindsay's level.

But there is something in sports known as "losing with dignity." Even the greatest fall short. Michael Jordan didn't win every basketball game while playing for the Chicago Bulls. But he still is considered one of the best to ever

Holding her 2000 Australian Open trophy cup, Lindsay gives a big thumbs-up to the cameras. She defeated first seed Martina Hingis in straight sets, 6-1 and 7-5, to take the title.

have laced up a pair of sneakers, mainly because he learned from his losses and came back stronger the next time.

The key to becoming a true winner is being able to handle the upsets and disappointments. That's true both on the court and off. Way before arriving at the 2001 Australian Open, life had taught Lindsay Davenport some very valuable lessons. She had to deal with moving to a new place and leaving behind her good friends. She took it hard when her parents divorced, but somehow she made it through that terrible time. And when her weight started to get out of control, Lindsay took it upon herself to get help and do something about it.

In other words, Lindsay used all of the setbacks in her life to develop character, which is one of the things that produces hope in an individual. So even losing big tournaments like the 2001 Australian Open are experiences she can handle. The reason Lindsay Davenport can do that is because she used life's lessons to learn how to cope with difficulty, instilling in her the remarkable ability to bounce back, just like a tennis ball.

STATISTICS

Source: Sanex WTA Tour

Year	Tournament	Round Reached	Prize Money
2001	Sydney	finals	$43,000
	Australian Open	semifinals	$115,875
	Pan Pacific	won	$175,000
	Scottsdale	won	$90,000
	Indian Wells	quarterfinals	$39,000
2000	Sydney	finals	$37,000
	Australian Open	won	$415,655
	Scottsdale	finals	$43,000
	Indian Wells	won	$330,000
	Miami	finals	$175,000
	Italian Open	round 16	$8,900
	French Open	round 128	$8,150
	Eastbourne	quarterfinals	$11,000
	Wimbledon	finals	$348,429
	Stanford	finals	$43,500
	San Diego	round 16	$7,600
	Los Angeles	finals	$43,500
	Du Maurier Open	round 16	$8,900
	U.S. Open	finals	$425,000
	Olympics—		
	Sydney, Australia	round 32	none
	Zurich	finals	$83,000
	Linz	won	$87,000
	Philadelphia	won	$87,000
	Chase Championship	round 16	$30,000
	Fed Cup Finals	round 5	$30,000
1999	Sydney	won	$64,000
	Australian Open	semifinals	$92,079
	Pan Pacific	quarterfinals	$18,500
	Indian Wells	round 32	$4,225
	Lipton	quarterfinals	$33,000
	Amelia Island	round 16	$4,400
	Madrid	won	$27,000
	French Open	quarterfinals	$75,647
	Wimbledon	won	$614,213
	Stanford	won	$80,000
	San Diego	semifinals	$20,000
	Los Angeles	semifinals	$20,000
	New Haven	finals	$40,000
	U.S. Open	semifinals	$210,000
	Fed Cup Finals	round 5	none
	Toyota Princess	won	$80,000

Year	Tournament	Round Reached	Prize Money
1999	Compaq Grand Slam	semifinals	$300,000
	Filderstadt	quarterfinals	$10,000
	Philadelphia	won	$10,000
	Chase Championships	won	$500,000
1998	Sydney	quarterfinals	$7,350
	Australian Open	semifinals	$107,196
	Pan Pacific	won	$150,000
	Oklahoma City	semifinals	$6,600
	Indian Wells	finals	$83,000
	Lipton	quarterfinals	$29,000
	Hilton Head	quarterfinals	$14,670
	Amelia Island	semifinals	$15,800
	Fed Cup	round 1	none
	German Open	round 16	$7,550
	French Open	semifinals	$151,400
	Wimbledon	quarterfinals	$78,961
	Stanford	won	$79,000
	San Diego	won	$79,000
	Los Angeles	won	$79,000
	New Haven	semifinals	$17,850
	U.S. Open	won	$700,000
	Grand Slam Cup	quarterfinals	$165,000
	Filderstadt	finals	$36,000
	Zurich	won	$150,000
	Philadelphia	finals	$36,000
	Chase Championships	finals	$250,000
1997	Sydney	semifinals	$13,900
	Australian Open	round 16	$29,226
	Pan Pacific	quarterfinals	$16,875
	Oklahoma City	won	$27,000
	Indian Wells	won	$205,000
	Lipton	round 16	$13,500
	Hilton Head	quarterfinals	$14,670
	Amelia Island	won	$79,000
	German Open	round 32	$2,640
	Strasbourg	round 16	$1,325
	French Open	round 16	$43,130
	Wimbledon	round 64	$12,576
	Fed Cup	round 2	none
	Stanford	semifinals	$17,850
	Los Angeles	finals	$36,000
	Du Maurier Open	quarterfinals	$14,670

Year	Tournament	Round Reached	Prize Money
1997	Atlanta	won	$79,000
	U.S. Open	semifinals	$175,000
	Filderstadt	round 16	$2,600
	Zurich	won	$150,000
	Chicago	won	$79,000
	Philadelphia	finals	$36,000
	Chase Championships	round 16	$24,720
1996	Sydney	finals	$26,500
	Australian Open	round 16	$22,621
	Pan Pacific	quarterfinals	$16,875
	Indian Wells	semifinals	$22,500
	Lipton	semifinals	$52,500
	Strasbourg	won	$27,000
	French Open	quarterfinals	$73,362
	Eastbourne	round 16	$3,925
	Wimbledon	round 64	$10,414
	Fed Cup	round 2	none
	Olympics—Atlanta	won	none
	Los Angeles	won	$80,000
	U.S. Open	round 16	$40,495
	Fed Cup	round 3	none
	Leipzig	quarterfinals	$10,000
	Filderstadt	semifinals	19,250
	Chicago	quarterfinals	$10,000
	Oakland	quarterfinals	$10,000
	Philadelphia	ound 32	$3,150
	Chase Championships	quarterfinals	$65,000
1995	Sydney	finals	$26,500
	Australian Open	quarterfinals	$38,457
	Pan Pacific	finals	$66,500
	Indian Wells	quarterfinals	$10,215
	Lipton	round 16	$12,330
	Strasbourg	won	$32,499
	French Open	round 16	$28,553
	Wimbledon	round 16	
	Fed Cup	round 2	none
	Los Angeles	quarterfinals	$7,980
	U.S. Open	round 64	$12,535
	Nichirei	quarterfinals	$9,325
	Leipzig	round 16	$2,570
	Filderstadt	round 16	$2,570
	Oakland	semifinals	$14,880
	Chase Championships	round 16	$30,0000

Year	Tournament	Round Reached	Prize Money
1994	Brisbane	won	$27,000
	Australian Open	quarterfinals	$40,413
	Chicago	quarterfinals	$9,600
	Indian Wells	semifinals	$18,000
	Lipton	semifinals	$37,500
	Houston	round 16	$5,050
	Hilton Head	quarterfinals	$15,000
	Amelia Island	semifinals	$16,000
	Lucerne	won	$27,000
	French Open	round 32	$16,091
	Wimbledon	quarterfinals	$50,363
	Fed Cup	round 5	none
	San Diego	quarterfinals	$6,050
	U.S. Open	round 32	$19,740
	Tokyo Nichirei	round 16	$4,600
	Oakland	semifinals	$20,000
	Philadelphia	round 16	$8,625
	Chase Championships	finals	$120,000
1993	Brisbane	round 16	$1,600
	Australian Open	round 32	$12,705
	Indian Wells	quarterfinals	$7,500
	Florida	quarterfinals	$7.500
	Lipton	round 64	$2,375
	Family Circle		
	Magazine Cup	round 32	$4,125
	Bausch & Lomb	round 16	$3,825
	European Open	won	$27,000
	French Open	round 128	$7,157
	Eastbourne	round 64	$1,025
	Wimbledon	round 32	$15,982
	Fed Cup	round 3	none
	Los Angeles	round 16	$3,825
	U.S. Open	round 16	$37,000
	Nichirei Tokyo	quarterfinals	$8,450
	Oakland	semifinals	$18,750
	Philadelphia	round 16	$8,625

CHRONOLOGY

1976	Lindsay Davenport is born on June 8 in Palos Verdes, California
1982	Lindsay begins playing tennis at age 6
1992	Competing in junior competition, Lindsay wins U.S. Open singles title
1993	After much success in amateur competition, Lindsay enters the professional ranks; One week after turning pro, Lindsay gets a stunning victory over Gabriela Sabatini, who was ranked No. 5 at the time; Lindsay's family moves to Murrieta, California
1994	With a B-plus average, Lindsay graduates from Murrieta Valley High School
1995	Lindsay's parents file for divorce; stressed out about her parents, Lindsay begins to overeat and gain weight; after getting up to 200 pounds, Lindsay commits to getting in shape
1996	Lindsay wins a gold medal at the Olympics
1998	After years of hearing that she could never win a major tennis tournament, Linsday captures the crown at the U.S. Open
1999	Lindsay beats tennis legend Steffi Graf to win her first Wimbledon championship
2000	Lindsay wins the Australian Open, her third Grand Slam title

FURTHER READING

Gilbert, Nancy. *Wimbledon.* Mankato, Minnesota: Creative Education, Inc., 1990.

Jensen, Julie. *Beginning Tennis.* Minneapolis: Lerner Publications Company, 1995.

Miller, Marc. *Fundamental Tennis.* Minneapolis: Lerner Publications Company, 1995.

Rutledge, Rachel. *The Best of the Best in Tennis (Women of Sports).* New York: Millbrook Press, 1998.

Schwabacher, Martin. *Superstars of Women's Tennis.* Philadelphia: Chelsea House Publishers, 1997.

Wade, Virginia. *Ladies of the Court: A Century of Women at Wimbledon.* New York: Atheneum, 1984.

INDEX

ABOUT THE AUTHOR

JOHN T. MCCANN is a writer currently working for the Orlando Sentinel in Orlando, Florida. He grew up in Raleigh, NC and earned a journalism degree from The University of North Carolina at Chapel Hill. His first newspaper job was in Durham, NC at The Herald-Sun, where he won a first-place award for commentary from the American Association of Sunday and Feature Editors in 1998.

John and his wife, Pamela, live in Winter Park, Florida.

HANNAH STORM, NBC Sports play-by-play announcer, reporter, and studio host, made her debut in 1992 at Wimbledon during the All England Tennis Championships. Shortly thereafter, she was paired with Jim Lampley to cohost the *Olympic Show* for the 1992 Olympic Games in Barcelona. Later that year, Storm was named cohost of *Notre Dame Saturday*, NBC's college football pregame show. Adding to her repertoire, Storm became a reporter for the 1994 Major League All-Star Game and the pregame host for the 1995, 1997, and 1999 World Series. Storm's success as host of *NBA Showtime* during the 1997–98 season won her the role as studio host for the inaugural season of the Women's National Basketball Association in 1998.

In 1996, Storm was selected as NBC's host for the Summer Olympics in Atlanta, and she has been named as host for both the 2000 Summer Olympics in Sydney and the 2002 Winter Olympics in Salt Lake City. Storm received a Gracie Allen Award for Outstanding Personal Achievement, which was presented by the American Women in Radio and Television Foundation (AWRTF), for her coverage of the 1999 NBA Finals and 1999 World Series. She has been married to NBC Sports broadcaster Dan Hicks since 1994. They have two daughters.
